COUNTRY LIVING

The Perfect Kitchen

COUNTRY LIVING

The Perfect Kitchen

Alexandra Parsons

HEARST BOOKS

A Division of Sterling Publishing Co., Inc.

NEW YORK

Library of Congress Cataloging-in-Publication Data

Parsons, Alexandra.
  Country living the perfect kitchen / Alexandra Parsons.
    p. cm.
  ISBN 1-58816-310-5
  1. Kitchens—Design and construction. I. Country living (New York, N.Y.) II. Title.
TX653 .P38 2004
643'.3—dc22

                                          2003057078

10 9 8 7 6 5 4 3 2 1

Published by Hearst Books
A Division of Sterling Publishing Co., Inc.
387 Park Avenue South, New York, NY 10016

For *Country Living*
Nancy Mernit Soriano, Editor-in-Chief
Lawrence A. Bilotti, Executive Editor
Pamela Mullen Abrahams, Senior Editor, Architecture and Home Building
Jennifer L. Vreeland, Editor, Architecture and Home Building

Country Living is a trademark owned by Hearst Magazines Property, Inc., in USA, and Hearst Communications, Inc., in Canada. Hearst Books is a trademark owned by Hearst Communications, Inc.

www.countryliving.com

Distributed in Canada by Sterling Publishing
c/o Canadian Manda Group, One Atlantic Avenue, Suite 105
Toronto, Ontario, Canada M6K 3E7

Distributed in Australia by Capricorn Link (Australia) Pty. Ltd.
P.O. Box 704, Windsor, NSW 2756 Australia

Manufactured in China

Designed by Christine Wood

ISBN 1-58816-310-5

Contents

Introduction

The country kitchen of today is a great deal more than a work space—it's a living room, a playroom, an office, a refuge, a dining room, and a hub of communications. In order to provide a reassuring and pleasurable backdrop to the ebb and flow of life, a kitchen needs to function well on all these levels.

More than any other room in the house, a kitchen requires forethought and preparation, whether you are designing a brand-new kitchen from scratch, remodeling an existing one, or just sprucing up parts of the kitchen. Thorough planning will enable you to create an attractive, high-performance kitchen that reflects your own priorities and personality. Achieving a successful balance between comfort, efficiency, and good looks is the secret of the perfect kitchen.

The aim of this book is twofold: to help you get the practicalities in order, and to inspire you with design ideas, so you can create a kitchen that works well for your lifestyle. There's no need to feel constrained—thanks to modern technology, most things are possible. The evocative feel of the farmhouse and the pleasurable associations of the country house kitchen today thankfully come with underfloor heating, space-age ventilation and refrigeration, and ranges providing industrial-grade efficiency at the touch of a button. It's time to let your dream kitchen take shape.

—Nancy Mernit Soriano
Editor-in-Chief, *Country Living*

CHAPTER ONE

Style and Function

The most obvious way to pick a design for your kitchen is to let the

type of home you live in be a major factor, but you must also consider

the life you lead. Busy people need small, efficient kitchens; dedicated

cooks, on the other hand, will want space to enjoy their art.

Planning a Kitchen That Works

However wonderful a kitchen looks, it is not going to make you happy unless it works for you and the life you lead. There is no point in decking out a magnificent cook's kitchen if all you ever do is blend a breakfast juice and order in a take-out meal. If you call upon professional help in the form of an architect or a Certified Kitchen Designer (C.K.D.), you will need to brief them thoroughly on your lifestyle and preferences. Knowing something of kitchen planning can help you to get the most from a professional planner. Taste is personal, but a well-designed space that works well for you is a reality, and a properly briefed designer can achieve it.

If you have young children, give yourself the best-equipped kitchen you can afford, but more importantly, give yourself space. Children will follow you wherever you go, so you will need floor and table space well away from the stove and sink.

If you have a growing family of snacking teenagers, you will probably find family harmony improved by having a separate snack preparation area, away from the main prepping and cooking zones, for sandwiches, cookies, and drinks.

If there are just two of you, it is worth making a pleasant dining area within the kitchen space, out of sight of the dirty dishes—for example, with a cleverly designed work island. But if you reduce your work area to a galley, remember that the gangway should be at least four feet wide if two people are to pass one another comfortably.

If you are single, avoid miniaturized kitchen fixtures that promise to maximize the available space for more sybaritic activities. Such dollhouse furnishings are both expensive and restricting.

If you love to cook and entertain, you will need an efficient, hardworking room planned and organized to the last detail, with special attention to ergonomics such as countertop heights. Allow for plenty of storage space, not only for food but also for your entire *batterie de cuisine*, kitchen gadgets, specialized equipment ranging from fish kettles to fine wire sieves, and all the plates, serving dishes, pitchers, glasses, candlesticks, tablecloths, and dish towels that you own or are likely to own. Do not imagine that calculating your present levels will suffice, because one thing is sure—you will acquire more.

ABOVE *The owner of this kitchen thought out everything carefully, even designing the cabinets herself to blend with the beaded-board walls. The work area is compact, but there's plenty of welcoming space for casual diners and helpers.*

11

The Work Sequence

The areas of a kitchen devoted to particular functions should ideally be arranged in the most efficient sequence—storage, preparation zone, sink, stove, serving area, and eating area—with dirty dishes returning along this path. The arrangement often becomes a triangle, which complies with the basic principle that should be behind all kitchen layouts: to reduce the number of unnecessary journeys.

Ergonomic studies have revealed that it is not the size of your kitchen that affects efficiency so much as the organization of the elements within. In most kitchens, activity centers around

ABOVE *A wooden countertop separates the dining area from the kitchen here. The copper food preparation sink positioned at the end of the counter means that there's no need to walk back into the kitchen to fill pitchers with water for the table.*

ABOVE *A view from the kitchen end of this well-planned cooking and eating space shows how work areas are linked by the center island. As well as housing the cooktop, this provides storage, a work surface for food prep, and a small snack bar, making good use of the generous space.*

the food storage area (refrigerator), the sink, and the stove. These key areas are linked by work surfaces used for food preparation and serving. By relating adjacent areas logically to one another in this way, and by limiting the total distance around the triangle to no more than 22 feet, the amount of walking you have to do is kept to a minimum. (However, anything less than 12 feet could make the space too cramped.) A kitchen designer can help you to plan this.

The starting point when planning your kitchen layout should be the sink since, with its attendant plumbing, it is the single most expensive and impractical item to move. The sink should be close to the cooktop, with generous work space on either side.

Good ventilation is essential, even in a kitchen with plenty of windows. Windows let fresh air in, but you need a vent hood to filter grease and suck cooking fumes out.

Cooking utensils that are regularly used do not have time to gather grease, so it's fine to display them near the stove.

Countertops of stainless steel are practical and easy to keep clean. Always use a chopping board to prevent scratches.

The path between the stove, refrigerator, and sink forms a triangle, with plenty of work space in between.

The top drawer in each base cabinet is the best place to store frequently used items.

Pans are kept in these drawers next to the stove.

Neither the sink nor the cooktop should be relegated to a corner—they need to be a good two feet from the side wall so that you don't bang your elbows, and so that you have a landing space on either side of these key areas. Avoid interrupting the work surface with housing for a built-in oven or a refrigerator. It's better to group these together at the end of the countertop.

For general food preparation, the countertop should be about two to four inches below the level of your elbow. The cooktop should be level with countertops on either side, and free-standing ranges are made to the same standard height as base cabinets (three feet). Ergonomic experts suggest the cooking zone should be about six inches lower than surfaces for preparation work so you can see into the pans. Ask your designer if this would be a good option for you. Countertop heights for base cabinets are generally three feet, which can be uncomfortable for anyone taller than average. Most cabinets have a plinth that is adjustable in increments of two inches, so check your comfort zone for chopping, mixing, and rinsing the dishes before the cabinets are installed. Many kitchens are designed with counters of different heights for different purposes—for example, a low section for tasks requiring some effort, such as mixing or pastry-making. This makes ergonomic sense but needs a critical eye to work aesthetically.

Vertical dimensions are also important considerations when planning storage. Bending down is more tiring that reaching up, and the farther you have to bend, the more floor space you will need. At each work station, plan for a top drawer or high shelf in base cabinets. On shelves and in wall cabinets, plan a shelf no higher than the height of the top of your head, so that you can see what you are doing without stretching.

Planning for Safety

RIGHT *Pan handles should never protrude and the spouts of boiling kettles should never point outward or at electric outlets.*

LEFT *One of the most common safety hazards is storing things just a little bit out of reach. A sturdy pair of steps is an ideal solution, useful for reaching into high cupboards and doubling as a step-up for young children eager to help with the dishes.*

Forty percent of all home accidents happen in the kitchen, which makes it by far the most dangerous room in the house. Most at risk are young children and the elderly, but carelessness can make statistics of us all. Your designer can help you plan to avoid potential hazards.

SAFETY ELEMENTS

● The cooktop is the most hazardous area of the kitchen. Do not install it beneath a wall cabinet, near billowing curtains or drying dish towels, or next to doors or windows that open. Allow space either side to land hot dishes.

● Fire is an ever-present hazard, so place a small foam fire extinguisher or fire blanket where you can easily find it. Never pour water on a fat fire—use the foam or fire blanket.

● If you have children, store sharp knives and caustic cleaners in locked cupboards or drawers. Childproof catches on cabinet doors and drawers and a guard rail on the cooktop will also make the kitchen safer for children.

● Never let steam discharge onto an electric socket. Install all switches and outlets well away from water. Do not overload electric outlets.

Windows and Light

A kitchen needs plenty of daylight, but not too much direct sunlight, which can cause glare and a buildup of heat. The ideal windows for the northern hemisphere will face east or north. It's not often that you can dictate where the windows are in your kitchen, however, and if your windows do face south or west, solar-control glass will help keep the room cool in the summer.

The position of a window, as well as its size, makes a significant difference to the amount of daylight entering the room. The higher the top of the window, the more light will stream into the room. Tall windows, skylights, or a glass roof will flood the whole kitchen with daylight. Strip windows set between the countertop and the wall cabinets will illuminate the countertop but little else, yet will be invaluable for shedding light on work areas. Positioning a sink under a window allows you to see out while you carry out your tasks.

Good lighting is vital in a kitchen, which is essentially a working environment. Supplementary sources of light will probably be necessary even during daylight hours. Having strongly contrasting pools of light and dark is not practical, but a bland overall lighting scheme makes the room look dull and formless, so aim for something between these two extremes.

RIGHT *Tall windows throw sunlight to the back of this classic kitchen. The light, airy feel is reinforced by soft, muted colors and open shelving.*

Task lighting and background lighting are both needed in the kitchen. Ask your designer for advice on choosing and fitting lighting. Counters, the sink, and the cooktop need to be evenly lit from above. Avoid positioning the light behind you, or you'll be working in your own shadow. Spotlights, under-cabinet strip lights, or well-positioned pendants can be used for this. For ambient lighting, downlights, track lighting, or wall-mounted uplights all work well, positioned so they wash pale walls or ceiling with light. The color of light depends on the type of lighting you choose. Fluorescent light can have a harsh, flattening effect, and it distorts color a little. Tungsten light is warmer in tone but emits a fair amount of heat. Halogen bulbs give a crisp, sparkly, white light; the low-voltage types are small and twinkly, whilst saving on electricity, but halogen does get very hot.

ABOVE *Sited directly above the work island, these stylish vintage-style pendants illuminate the counter and sink. In addition, they add to the ambient lighting provided by the recessed downlights.*

RIGHT *The best natural light comes from above—which is why tall windows work so well. Here a windowless wall is lit from above by skylights.*

Ambient lighting comes from a row of pendants positioned over the 1860s Dutch table, which serves as a work island.

Low-voltage track lighting over the work surface floods the countertop with even light.

A bank of windows above the sink and countertop lets the sun shine in and gives a panoramic view of the garden. The windows each pivot on a central vertical axis, making them easy to nudge open and position for ventilation while keeping out wind or rain.

The multi-paned door adds to the incoming light. When sunlight enters a room from two directions, light is diffused and softened and glare is reduced.

LEFT *Throughout this house, sliding glass doors open wide, embracing the view of the lake and the light reflected off it. From the kitchen the cook enjoys the wonderful views and diners feel they are eating at the lakeside. Simple matchstick blinds keep out the glare by day and provide some privacy by night.*

ABOVE LEFT *The sink was placed under the large window overlooking the yard. Many hours are spent at the sink, and an outlook like this is much more interesting than a blank wall. It is also useful to keep an eye on young children playing in the yard.*

ABOVE RIGHT *Daylight falls obliquely onto the range. A light in the vent hood illuminates the cooktop, making it easier to see what you are doing.*

LEFT *Tiny potted ivies nestle on narrow shelves that are aligned with the horizontal glazing bars. The herbs on the countertop enjoy a first-rate growing environment.*

RIGHT *Oversize, multi-paned windows flood this kitchen with natural light. The opening casement behind the sink lets the garden into the kitchen, and vice versa, making the sink area a very pleasant place to work.*

Ventilation

Good ventilation is vital, and not just for the comfort of the cook. Steam, fumes, and grease-laden air can play havoc with structural timbers and ruin the décor. Extractor fans and open windows help, but the cooktop requires something drastic. The best system is a vent hood that sucks up heat, smoke, fat, and steam, then filters it and ejects it outside. The alternatives are a hood that filters the air before recirculating it into the room and a downdraft system built into the cooktop that sucks up steam and fumes at the source and ducts them to the outside.

Sinks

LEFT *In a kitchen filled with period details and personal collections, a 1920s ceramic sink has been lovingly restored. The hand-held faucet is perfect for rinsing vegetables and the hinged copper drainer is as efficient as it is good-looking.*

RIGHT *A tall swan-neck faucet makes filling tall pots easy, while the retractable hand spray can be used for rinsing dishes.*

If you consider the number of kitchen activities that require water, from pan-filling to washing food and dishes (not to mention waste disposal), you will come to the inevitable conclusion that one sink is not enough. If you have the space, consider installing a small food-rinsing and pan-filling sink near the cooktop and a generous-size sink elsewhere. A well-designed, large, multipurpose single sink can offer more flexibility than a double sink, as it can accommodate baking sheets and large pans and offers the option of accessories like a draining rack, colander basket, or chopping board that can be slotted in when required. Ask your designer if an extra sink can be incorporated.

The material will be dictated by the style of your kitchen. Stainless steel is streamlined, hygienic, and long-lasting; vitreous enamel can add color. Solid surfacing sinks offer a colorful, seamless look, while large ceramic, stone, or even wood sinks add a traditional country touch.

KITCHEN ELEMENTS: SINKS AND FAUCETS

Dishwashers have made large sinks with long expanses of drainer redundant.

1 Twin-bowl sinks allow you to wash and rinse dishes and even laundry while the other bowl is in use. Self-rimming sinks sit just above the countertop and are sealed with a waterproof edge. They are easy to install and very popular.

2 A traditional country sink is deep, wide, and has the depth to wash large pots and pans. With an undermounted sink there are no joins to harbor germs. Another hygenic option are sleek-looking solid-surfacing materials in which the sink is an integral part of the drainer or counter.

3 Faucets must be easy to turn on and off. Lever-style controls with a single mixer spigot are one of the best combinations. Kitchen faucets can be either wall-mounted or surface-mounted.

4 In a large kitchen you can include an extra sink dedicated to food preparation fitted with a waste-disposal unit.

5 This generous apron-fronted double sink has been housed in a cabinet that resembles a Victorian washstand.

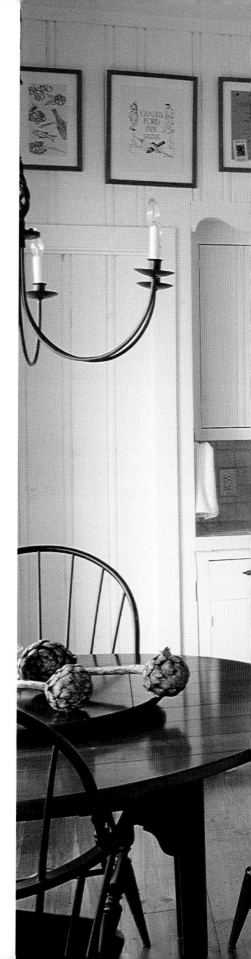

LEFT *Granite and slate look sleek and modern as well as being hygienic and waterproof (though slate has to be sealed).*

RIGHT *This homey kitchen benefits from a variety of countertops. An economical white laminate covers the countertop on either side of the sink. An old-fashioned butcher block work station is the ideal spot to chop vegetables, and the base cabinets facing the dining area are smartly topped with ceramic tiles.*

Countertops

A great deal is demanded of the average kitchen work surface—it must withstand the heat of pots and pans, the cutting edges of knives, assaults with abrasive cleaners, and constant dousings of soapy water. But as there is no one perfect surface, compromise is inevitable.

Because each type of worktop has particular advantages and disadvantages (see page 35), it makes sense to use different materials in different activity zones. For example, a heat-proof surface such as granite or stainless steel could be used adjacent to the cooktop, and a waterproof material like stainless steel or solid surfacing would be good as a draining board.

Chopping is perhaps the one kitchen activity than no surface particularly likes. Therefore, equip yourself with several chopping boards made from end-grain wood. Although polypropylene was once regarded as the most hygienic of chopping surfaces, the natural anti-bacterial qualities of wood are now recognized, making wooden chopping boards unbeatable.

1

KITCHEN ELEMENTS: MATERIALS FOR COUNTERS

1 Laminates are easy to keep clean and relatively inexpensive, but they scratch easily and are not completely heat-proof. They come in a huge range of colors, patterns, and textures.

2 Marble is cool, beautiful, and expensive. It is ideal for pastry-making. Oil or harsh spirits will stain it.

3 Stainless steel is hygienic and hard-wearing. It withstands extreme heat, but scratches easily.

OTHER SUITABLE MATERIALS

Hardwood is attractive and hard-wearing, but needs frequent cleaning and resealing. Very hot pans can leave marks.

Slate is hard-wearing and waterproof once it has been sealed—but it scratches easily.

Ceramic tiles are waterproof and stain- and heat-resistant, but prone to cracking. Ceramic surfaces are noisy, will blunt knives, and the grout may discolor over time.

Pure granite, the hardest stone, is waterproof, stain- and scratch-resistant, and heat-proof, but expensive. Granite work surfaces are also available as composites of crushed granite and quartz, which can be more affordable, but still retain granite's hard-wearing properties.

Solid surfacing materials can be formed into any shape, so the sink and countertop can be molded out of one piece. Made from polyester or acrylic resins, they are available in many colors, and are heat- and stain-resistant, but they are expensive and must be professionally installed.

Cast concrete is hard-wearing and heat-resistant. It is expensive, as it has to be cast on site.

Walls and Backsplashes

Kitchen walls see a lot of activity, as they are subjected to hot, steamy conditions as well as water splashes, grease splatters, and food spillages. It's essential, therefore, that they are easy to wipe clean—the kitchen is not the place for fancy wallpapers, though vinyl wallcoverings can be used. In fact, the wall finishes can be as varied as you like, depending on the style of your kitchen, from beaded-board paneling or exposed brick to the new breed of tough, washable paint finishes, which withstand condensation.

The backsplash, which runs just above the countertops, should be tough and durable. Behind the cooktop it needs to be heat-resistant, and behind the sink totally waterproof. The backsplash could be in the same material as the counter, but a contrasting material can look good. It must, however, be practical. Ceramic, slate, marble tiles, toughened glass (fused with another material to prevent breaking), stainless steel, and copper will all fulfill this role and retain their good looks.

LEFT *In a sunny kitchen with a classic feel, pale blue walls provide a cool, streamlined backdrop for a collection of framed botanical prints and a row of simple, painted chairs.*

RIGHT *Wood paneling adds to the atmosphere of a cozy country kitchen, though it isn't practical unless it has been sealed.*

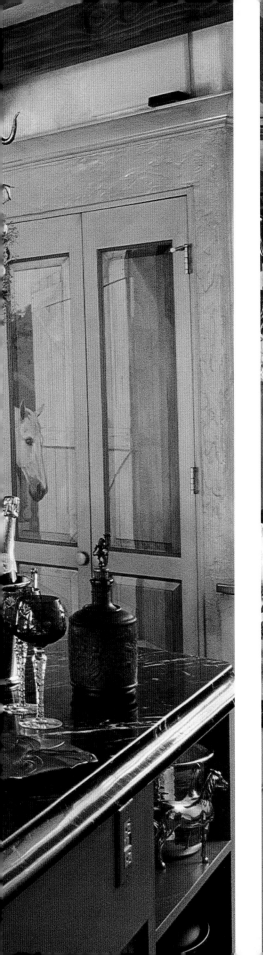

FAR LEFT *As an antidote to the conventional immaculate, all-white look, this kitchen has a colorful animal theme, and it was all done with paint. The walls and ceiling have been glazed to suggest the rubble of antique plaster.*

LEFT *A large cast-iron cooktop and range is tucked into an alcove at the far end of the kitchen. The wall within the alcove is sensibly covered with easy-to-clean ceramic tiles.*

LEFT *The warm wood tones of this kitchen are echoed in the wood flooring, which has been stained to resemble checkerboard tiling. The diagonal lines make the room seem bigger.*

RIGHT *In a kitchen that uses paint effects to imitate the attractive patina imparted by a century of use, painted "rugs" define the work area.*

Floors

All kitchen flooring is subject to hard wear, so you have to pick a durable surface that is resistant to household chemicals, is easy to clean, and is not going to stain or warp when the dishwasher floods or a bottle of wine slips out of your fingers.

Wood is warm and resilient underfoot, but it will need regular attention, and possibly resealing from time to time. Softwoods can be stained or painted very successfully, but scuffing will eventually wear away a paint finish. Solid hardwoods, though expensive, will keep their good looks longer, so the extra outlay may be worth it in the long run. Seal wooden floors with polyurethane; wax polish is not advisable for kitchen floors because it can make wood slippery and it stains when damp.

LEFT *Vinyl is the best choice for family life as it is functional, stain-resistant, and comfortable underfoot. It comes in tile or sheet form in hundreds of designs and colors.*

RIGHT *A retro-style kitchen full of bright color and period pieces has a cheerful floor of 12-inch vinyl tiles in a checkerboard pattern.*

Ceramic, terra-cotta, and terrazzo tiles and marble, slate, granite, or limestone tiles or slabs make beautiful floors that will last a lifetime. However, they are expensive and are hard and cold to the touch, so they may also be unadvisable if you have young children. Underfloor heating will help warm them up. Many are porous and must be sealed.

Cork, vinyl, linoleum, and rubber are warm and resilient underfoot. Vinyl, in sheet form or in tiles, is probably the most popular kitchen flooring material, and there's a vast range of colors, patterns, and textures, ranging from the sophisticated to the whimsical. These surfaces are quite forgiving if you drop something, and so are also a good choice for young families.

ABOVE *Quarry tiles link the kitchen to the dining area and are a practical solution for both.*

A checkerboard tile pattern painted onto wooden boards defines the kitchen area. Painted floors need several coats of polyurethane sealant.

Following the removal of the wall between the kitchen and sun room, the change in floor surfaces is delineated with a black border strip.

Irregular stone flags cover the floor of the adjacent eating area.

You can opt for the best of both worlds if your kitchen is large enough to accommodate two floor finishes. You may prefer a surface that is both kind to the feet and waterproof in the working part of the kitchen and something more refined for the eating area—perhaps a finish that will complement flooring used in adjacent rooms.

If you choose tiled flooring, bear in mind that generous-size spaces look best with large, plain, matte tiles such as limestone flags or terra-cotta. If you have a small or narrow kitchen, use tiles to play with perspective. For example, laying them on the diagonal will make the room seem larger and wider.

LEFT *A retro-style enameled stove has plenty of pan parking space around the outside of the burners. A stove with four hotplates on the top and one or two ovens underneath is the most cost-effective of all cooking appliances. Installing a freestanding stove costs a great deal less than installing separate components which each require their own fireproof casing.*

Ovens and Cooktops

Most cooks have very specific preferences when it comes to cooktops. Some prefer gas, while others swear by electricity, but there are so many options available now—from freestanding, pro-style, stainless steel models to unobtrusive ceramic halogen cooktops—it can be hard to focus on what really suits you and the life you lead. Explain your priorities to your designer before making a decision so you won't be seduced by good looks.

Manufacturers now offer cooktop components such as built-in griddles, steamers, deep-fat fryers, and wok burners. If your cooking demands it, they might come in handy. Just remember that it can get very expensive to overestimate your cooking needs.

ABOVE LEFT *A blend of old and new: a state-of-the-art stainless steel range slotted into traditional cabinetry and a high-level shelf displaying a collection of Victorian ironstone. Custom wood drawers that fit into cubbyholes above the range keep cooking utensils conveniently close to the action.*

ABOVE RIGHT *A ceramic halogen cooktop comes close to providing the speed and versatility of gas.*

A stove with a single oven and a cooktop, known as a slide-in, is ideal for a small kitchen, but if you have the space, a separate cooktop and a built-in oven will give you more flexibility. Eye-level ovens are safer and easier to load than those below counter level.

Many built-in ovens come with a double-oven option, which is ideal for the enthusiastic cook. If you do less baking and roasting you could substitute a microwave for the second oven.

Pro-style ranges, in stainless steel or enamel, are excellent for the country kitchen. They come in various sizes from 30-inch units to 60-inch models with six-burners, a hotplate, and two ovens, which are wonderful if you have a large family. A pro-style range heats more quickly than a domestic model, but may require special ventilation and a strong foundation. Check with your designer.

KITCHEN ELEMENTS: COOKTOPS AND OVENS

1 Wall-mounted double ovens offer a choice of functions, such as a microwave or convection oven. They can be installed at a convenient height to reduce the amount of bending required.

2 Slide-in pro-style gas stoves, with cast-iron pot stands on the cooktop, are as much at home in traditional settings as they are in a sea of professional stainless steel. Pro-style ranges tend to be more heavy-duty than freestanding versions, with powerful burners and heavy-duty knobs and grates.

3 Traditionally, electricity has been the fuel of choice for ovens, as it offers more even temperatures and easier cleaning. However, gas ovens are becoming more competitive. A conventional electric oven is hotter at the top than the bottom because hot air rises, so they are they first choice for soufflés or delicate cakes. Ovens with a convection mode use a fan to circulate warm air around the oven, cooking more evenly and quicker than non-fan options, but fans can be bulky, reducing the capacity of the oven.

4 Separating the cooktop from the oven offers flexibility—both to position your cooktop and oven where you wish and to choose the fuels. A separate cooktop also allows you to choose optional elements such as extra burners or griddles. Some freestanding stoves combine gas cooktops with electric ovens. For cooktops, gas offers greater precision than electricity. You can see the size of the flame, and shut off the heat instantly. Electric elements heat faster than gas, and cooktops can be smooth for easy cleaning. Halogen offers the instant heat of gas, but with a smooth cooktop and intense heat. However, not all cookware is suitable for halogen.

Cabinets and Storage

Efficient storage makes for a kitchen that is a pleasure to work in. Do your own kitchen arrangements make sense? If you stretch out your hand from the cooktop, are your pans, wooden spoons, and seasonings right there, just where you want them? Standing by the chopping board, can you reach all your knives? Are the potholders within reach of the oven and are plates and silverware stored conveniently close to the dishwasher? All it takes to get it right is logic and careful planning. Make sure your designer knows exactly how you use your kitchen.

Be ruthless, and take out of the kitchen everything that does not deserve to be there, from vacuum cleaners to dog baskets and ironing boards. The space required for cooking and dining equipment, not to mention food storage, will always be greater than you think, and extraneous items should be banned from the equation.

LEFT *Some things are too good to hide away in cupboards. In this case it is a nineteenth-century English Spode pitcher with a bouquet of vintage Bakelite-handled knives.*

RIGHT *In this beach house, the kitchen shelves are stacked with inexpensive glassware and mismatched china, making an ever-changing display.*

A good storage system marries practicality with decorative display. This shelf is at a good height for someone working at the range to reach, and it's the ideal place for frequently used seasonings that would otherwise clutter up the countertop.

Wine is best stored in a cool (60°F), well-ventilated cellar. Temperature-controlled units like this are the next best thing. If you store wine in simple wire or wooden racks, position them as far from the stove as possible; otherwise the variation in temperature will ruin the wine.

Open shelves mean that you can see everything at a glance, which makes them ideal for everyday tableware, cookbooks, and the like. The shelves under this work island are shallow on the side facing the dining area, so nothing is hidden at the back. The other side of the island has deep pull-out drawers for pan storage. It is possible to put shelves on runners, too, creating giant pull-out trays, which are easy to access, especially for storage below counter height.

To organize your kitchen storage successfully, it pays to be disciplined. Only objects used every day, or at least once a week, deserve prime storage space within easy reach— somewhere between knee and eye level. Store party platters and silver candlesticks on the top shelves or at the back of low cupboards. Glass doors allow you to survey the contents of your cupboard shelves at a glance, particularly if you stack them for display.

1

2

3

4

KITCHEN ELEMENTS: CUPBOARDS AND CABINETS

1, 3, 4 Glass-fronted kitchen cupboards can become cabinets of curiosities, making them a design feature. You do not have to rely on pretty china for this effect—displays of antique kitchen equipment such as cookie cutters, storage jars, and tea caddies can be as effective.

2 Plain cabinet doors can be embellished. These units have been transformed using paint effects to make them look like finely veneered and inlaid cabinets.

5 Glass-fronted cabinet doors look great, create a light, airy feel in the kitchen, and also allow you to show off any collections of china, glassware or other items you may have.

6 Silverware trays do the job adequately, but all too often the compartments are too narrow, too long, or too short. Choose several trays with different-sized compartments. That way, even the least-used items in the drawer can be easily located.

6

5

Storing Food

Refrigerators and freezers are, of course, at the forefront when it comes to making perishable items last longer, but they don't solve every problem. Some foods, such as soft cheeses, eggs, and root vegetables, are best kept in a cool, dark cupboard instead. The argument for including a custom-built pantry in your kitchen plans is just as valid as it was a hundred years ago.

Cupboards should be dry, well-ventilated, and not too close to sources of heat. They are the ideal place to keep not just canned foods but also dry goods such as flour and sugar.

Pantries are a wonderful addition to a kitchen, particularly the walk-in type, which was traditionally large enough to store bread bins, cases of wine, and flagons of olive oil on cool marble or tile shelves. This type of pantry was built against the coolest outside wall of the kitchen and had vents, fly-proofed with thin gauze, to create a flow of cold air. A pantry should have sturdy shelves and cupboards and good lighting. If you have the space a sink could be useful.

If you don't have a walk-in pantry, ask your designer if you can install vents into the coolest wall at the back of the kitchen cabinets to allow the cool air to circulate. Fit the cabinets with wire baskets or shelves in order to keep the cool air flowing.

LEFT *While some refrigerator-freezers are disguised with panels that match the cabinet doors so they blend anonymously into a range of cupboards, others, like this handsome stainless steel model, announce their presence and invite further inspection.*

RIGHT *This temperature-controlled wine cabinet stores bottles of red wine at an optimum 60°F. The racks are on runners—you just pull out a rack and tilt it down to make your selection.*

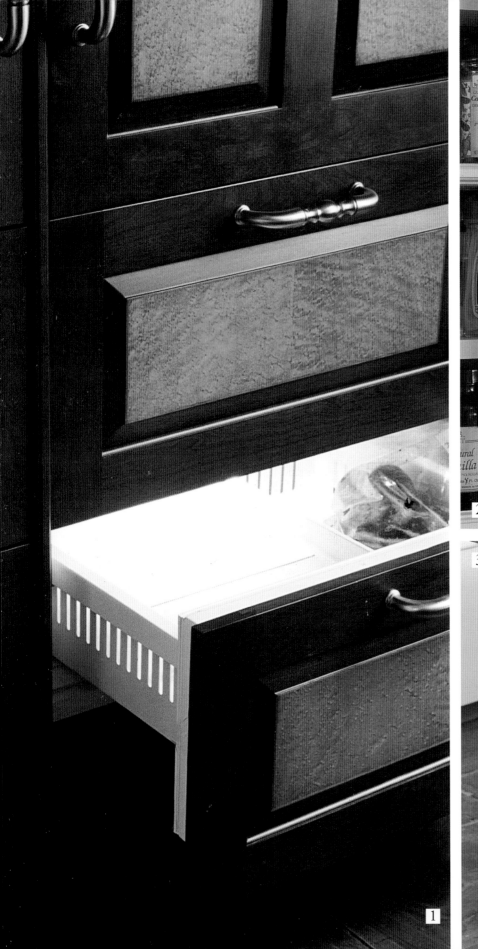

KITCHEN ELEMENTS: STORAGE OPTIONS

1 Refrigerator drawers that you can really see into are a practical idea as they help avoid the problem of food becoming forgotten at the back of the refrigerator.

2 Jars and cans often have attractive labels that can look like little works of art if arranged creatively behind glass doors. Store them on narrow shelves so that you won't forget the ones at the back of the cupboard.

3 Food storage should be related to cooking habits, and cupboards should be regularly edited. Spices and dried herbs in particular quickly lose their pungency and should routinely be replaced.

4 The alternative to the ubiquitous kitchen storage canister for dry goods is a glass-fronted drawer. Many health food stores display their legumes and grains in this way. At home you do not have to fill the drawer—a divider will keep an attractive amount visible from the front and allow you to cram in any number of half-finished packages at the back.

CHAPTER TWO

Kitchen Style

A country kitchen evokes a welcoming and wholesome environment,

and there are many different interpretations within the genre—from

modern, clean, and uncluttered to cozy, retro chic. The beautiful kitchens

photographed in this section will inspire you to turn your ideas and

preferences into a pleasing, personal style.

Traditional Country

Associated with the solid values of brick, wood, and other natural materials, this style is epitomized by the large, generous kitchen furnished with country antiques and decorated with country arts and crafts. All in all, it is a comforting place to be.

Simplicity and function are the keys to this welcoming style. Keep the color palette natural. For a really authentic look chalky whitewash looks great, but you could use shades of cream or beige, or even rich terracotta for a cosier feel. When looking for natural materials, try using local timber or stone, just as your ancestors would have done. What could be more welcoming than a generous-size wooden table or a hutch made from locally produced materials?

Cheerful clutter is very much a part of this look. The natural activities of the kitchen provide their own stylish decoration—a cluster of traditional cooking utensils, bunches of drying herbs, and a string of onions or garlic really say "country". To help the mood along hide up-to-date electronic equipment in cabinets or drawers and display pretty plates and cups on open shelves.

RIGHT *The walls of this mountain cabin are clad throughout in beaded-board wainscoting, and the simple kitchen cupboards blend in perfectly. Antique tables have been used for the central work station and the sink unit against the far wall. Decoration is restricted to a collection of old tin kitchen and farm tools that make a pleasing pattern on the wall.*

LEFT *The relaxed dining area of the cabin has a full wall of windows to welcome in views, sunlight, and fresh air. The solid country dining table has thick, turned legs and an easy-to-maintain zinc top.*

A Federal-style house has been transformed with wide open spaces. The atmospheric kitchen was made by combining several tiny rooms and an attic above them. Now a light-filled space, it has become a center of activity. The hand-crafted cabinets of rich cherry wood and the witch's-elbow fireplace, which was built with mellow old bricks, give the room its comforting feeling of warmth.

ABOVE *The pair of authentic 1850s French doors flanking the mantelpiece open onto a cedar deck. The floor is made of reclaimed yellow-pine planks and the hearth is of bluestone.*

ABOVE *The kitchen reflects a sense of history everywhere you look, from the nineteenth-century American kitchen chairs to the apothecary drawers built with the cabinets and based on antique designs.*

The granite-topped work island houses a sink, dishwasher, and wine cooler, and provides ample storage. Beautifully crafted wall cabinets hide all the cooking necessities not intended for display, while traditional dishware and utilitarian kitchen antiques have pride of place, adding to the room's timeless charm. It's all in the details: The cabinets themselves feature nineteenth-century touches such as raised panels and elegant crown moldings.

RIGHT *This wonderfully rambling country kitchen was deliberately designed with no single focal point. Instead, each work or storage area is defined by French antiques. An oak and pine butcher block is the centerpiece of the baking zone, a farm table completes the food prep island, and sheaf-back chairs encircle the dining area. A thick slab of granite was used for the raised hearth.*

LEFT *A detail of the well-worn butcher block, adorned with copperware and candy molds. A slot for knives runs along the back of the block.*

LEFT *Country touches in the flower room cum pantry of a Beaux-Arts mansion in New York. The shelves beneath the sink are curtained off with fresh green gingham.*

ABOVE LEFT *Delicate antique wire salad shakers are a suitably whimsical touch.*

ABOVE RIGHT *Ideal textiles for display in the traditional country kitchen are well-ironed lace-edged cotton and antique linen hand towels.*

To inject a dash of color into traditional country decor, choose simple patterns such as small prints that reflect the forms of nature, or use fresh cotton ginghams, tickings, or plaids to brighten the place up. It is unlikely that you would want to hang framed pictures in a traditional country kitchen, but you can still create a colorful or decorative focal point using traditional household linens. Simply tack them to the wall or hang them over wooden rails. You could also display a pretty vintage lace collar in a simple wooden frame.

When choosing decorative textiles for your kitchen, think along the lines of flour sacks rather than needlepoint, ethnic throws rather than silk wall hangings, and braided or woven rag rugs rather than contemporary rugs. The simpler the better.

Not all your choices have to be traditional or antique pieces—with this eclectic style the most important thing is to choose pieces that you love.

A traditional country kitchen will ideally have original architectural details. The owners decided to keep the original beaded-board wainscoting, the wall cabinets over the sink, and the large double-hung windows. Once these basic bones were restored, the decoration and furnishing could begin.

Antiques and a pretty fern wallpaper capture the feeling of the surrounding gardens.

Glass-fronted cabinets add to the traditional country feel, particularly if you fill them with old-fashioned containers.

A slender open shelf behind the farmhouse sink is full of reassuring country touches including a pot of ivy, a pretty dish, and a handful of frequently used cookbooks. Urban minimalists would have none of these.

A cottage-style work peninsula was built in the same idiom as the existing cabinetry. It turns a large room into an efficient galley kitchen and provides vital countertop space without sacrificing the windows.

White paint and colorful ceramic tableware lighten and brighten the room.

There is ample storage space in the peninsula and surrounding cupboards for cookware and clutter, leaving the countertops free for tempting displays of fruits and flowers.

LEFT *Calm simplicity and candlelight create the atmosphere of stillness so typical of the Shaker interior. The main decorations are food and flowers.*

RIGHT *Sunlight streaming through shutters gives this interior an almost painterly quality. The simple display of beautifully made utilitarian objects above the door is a typically Shaker touch.*

Shaker

Every object the Shakers made was beautifully crafted, plain and simple to use, functional, and built to last. It is a very appealing style for kitchens, where functionality is as much of a priority as good looks.

Many modern kitchen cabinets are dubbed "Shaker style" if they have plain wooden pulls and knobs, but it takes more than that to achieve the sense of calm and order at the root of true Shaker style. A very uncluttered look, it incorporates white, unadorned walls; natural materials such as wood, quarry tile, stone, or brick for flooring; well-crafted cabinetry; simple, clean-lined wooden countertops; a cast iron range and a ceramic sink; and only the bare minimum of kitchen implements on display.

The simple country look that we associate with Shaker style is becoming ever more popular, along with the idea of the kitchen as a gathering room at the heart of the home where all are welcome. A timeless look, Shaker style has a pared-down simplicity of line that blends perfectly with the latest kitchen fittings and equipment. Modern varnishes and sealants make natural wood, slate, and stone more easy to care for, and therefore a practical choice for a busy modern kitchen.

RIGHT *Ample storage in paneled wooden cabinets was a key feature of Shaker kitchens. Soapstone countertops and open shelves supported by custom brackets add to the traditional look of this kitchen. The cream-colored cabinetry speaks of a no-nonsense sensibility, while the hand-woven rug is a tribute to simple home crafts.*

BELOW *A simple, light-filled kitchen with a comfortingly timeless feel. The wood plank table at the heart of this room is used for food preparation and for dining.*

The exposed beams are part of the eighteenth-century structure of this warm and welcoming country kitchen.

The clean-lined cabinetry has compartments for books, spices, and gadgets, improving the kitchen's efficiency while furthering the traditional American ambience.

An off-white beaded-board backsplash helps to brighten the room and show off the cheerful red cabinets. Homemakers were not afraid of color in the eighteenth century.

The soapstone countertops and deep farmhouse sink make a strong, simple statement.

A neat, clutter-free solution for dish towels, the wooden rack slides back into a custom-made narrow opening.

The wide-plank pine floors are original. They had been hidden beneath linoleum for decades before being restored.

BELOW *The lights hanging over the work island in this renovated kitchen are industrial bakery lights. They are completely enclosed and therefore easy to wash. A built-in window seat spans the length of the new multi-paned picture window that floods the kitchen with natural light.*

Modern Country

This style is really traditional country that has embraced modern elements. It is epitomized by generous, open spaces, but there's a dash of cutting-edge style evident in its leaner lines and the addition of some sophisticated elements, such as state-of-the-art appliances and gadgets.

Combining a sense of warmth and comfort with innovation, the style juxtaposes traditional style and architectural features with modern professional materials like stainless steel, cast concrete, and lava-stone.

LEFT *A smart country kitchen that is well planned, well lit, and well used. The mix of materials—the painted wood, pristine stainless steel, reclaimed chestnut floorboards, and durable lava-stone countertop—reflects this kitchen's modern sensibilities.*

RIGHT *The architecture of this newly built country retreat pays homage to rustic farm buildings. Southern pine salvaged from old barns and factories was recycled to make the interior trusses, the flooring, and the kitchen cabinets. The pot racks of hand-forged steel suit the barn-like atmosphere. The work island's cast-concrete countertop was impregnated with a blue pigment to make it stand out against the natural tones of wood and plaster.*

LEFT *This is an excellent example of having the best of both worlds. Clutter is hidden in cabinets that merge visually with the wall, and decorative kitchen items are displayed in a practical way close to the point of use.*

RIGHT *Hanging pots and pans with cast-iron bases are as attractive as they are useful.*

FAR RIGHT *Frosted cabinet doors conceal and reveal at the same time.*

Cool, white light and a lack of clutter lend a distinct feeling of spaciousness that accords well with the modern country feel. Kitchens such as these are places where family and guests meet to talk and to help with food preparation—a work island with plenty of bar stools encourages this gregarious habit.

Skylights have given this kitchen the injection of daylight that it needed, and the white-painted paneled walls and cabinets bounce the light into every corner. The cooktop and ovens are made of stainless steel but their finishes are more subdued and their contours more rounded than those of many industrial-looking modern appliances. The countertops are a dark polished concrete that looks and feels surprisingly traditional.

The colorful touch comes from an interesting textile.

Windows are left bare—a good idea so near the range. Privacy is rarely an issue in a kitchen.

The uncluttered cooking area is efficient, and a wide vent hood whisks away steam and smells from the range.

Countertops are made from old wide plank floorboards, sanded and sealed to make them splashproof and hygienic.

The breakfast bar on the central island is higher than the prepping area, effectively hiding the sink from the dining area.

The work area is paved with recycled, mellow old bricks.

ABOVE LEFT AND RIGHT *A traditional country sink is set into a granite countertop. Granite and slate are perfect materials for the modern country look.*

Unusual surfaces give a kitchen character. For a modern country kitchen, a wonderful assortment of colors and textures is available within the range of natural materials, along with a wide selection of seals and stains to make them practical and beautiful.

For countertops, experiment with textural juxtapositions such as polished concrete with wood or tonal contrasts such as cool white marble with steely gray granite. Floors can also benefit from a bit of mixing and matching. Wood is a wonderful surface, especially with underfloor heating, but it is not particularly practical near water, so an inset tiled area or a patch of flagstones or well-worn old bricks could do the trick. Plain painted walls could benefit both practically and aesthetically from a backsplash of glass, stainless steel, or glazed tile.

LEFT *These base cabinets are designed to appear old— distressed edges on the black doors and drawers simulate the effects of years of use. The countertops are made of polished cast concrete and the floor is boarded with reclaimed planks.*

RIGHT *A kitchen that works both practically and aesthetically. The stainless steel double sink next to the cooktop is for food preparation and filling pans. On the back wall the integrated single sink with draining board is used for rinsing dishes.*

In this thoughtful renovation, the kitchen addition has been linked to the rest of the house, and old and new live seamlessly side by side. The accoutrements of a serious cook's kitchen—modern appliances such as a stainless steel oven and an efficient gas cooktop—have been successfully integrated with more traditional elements, such as cabinets painted with a distressed finish and a reclaimed-wood floor. The glass-fronted wall cabinets are filled with traditional country-style bowls and pitchers. They are finished with elegant supports that define space on the polished concrete countertop dedicated to decorative storage containers.

LEFT *This inviting kitchen offers plenty of space for every conceivable kitchen activity, from baking to tackling homework. The relaxed country feel belies a host of practical modern features.*

BELOW *With creamy white walls and windows on all three sides, this kitchen is bathed in light. Fully fitted cabinets in a sturdy country style are topped with stone countertops for a look that is clean, crisp, and classic, but with a modern layout, and without the 'busyness' of the traditional country kitchen. The central island functions as a work area and storage unit, incorporating a dishwasher and a recycling center and there is no attempt to hide the state-of-the-art appliances. It's a brand-new kitchen with a gently evocative feel of the past.*

Retro

LEFT *Reproductions of vintage appliances are at the core of this kitchen's retro charm. The maple cabinets are equipped with porcelain knobs to emphasize the white enamel. Green and white ceramic tiles form a checkerboard pattern on the floor.*

RIGHT *This is a case of a kitchen built around a passion for Fire-King oven-to tableware. If you choose a theme such as this, you have to be very sure that your passions will endure.*

This quirky and fun country style is about total immersion in the 1940s and '50s—an era when domesticity was at its height, pastels were the colors of choice, with zinging highlights of green or red, product packaging was in its exuberant infancy, and enameled curves were to die for.

Accessorizing the retro kitchen can become addictive. Flea markets and thrift stores yield a treasure trove of well-crafted kitchen utensils, jazzy crockery in crazy colors, and Bakelite knickknacks. In fact, a collection of these items is often the starting point, inspiring its owners to explore further and create an authentic showcase for their Jade-Ite bowls or their enamelware ewers and bread bins. Manufacturers have caught on to this trend, and it is possible now to buy practical modern kitchen appliances built along retro lines. After the fashion for clean minimalism, it is perhaps time for the pendulum to swing back to the days of curves, chrome, and primary colors.

Kitchen displays are an invitation to enjoy and appreciate the beauty of everyday things. For the owner of a retro kitchen, this means striking a balance between running a museum and creating a practical work space that suits lifestyle and cooking habits. The best way to achieve this is to use the items in the collection on a day-to-day basis rather than treat them with reverence in glass cabinets. Eat off those colorful Bakelite™ plates, get that old toaster and kitchen mixer refurbished and rechromed, pop the Pyrex™ into the Magic Chef™ stove, and live the retro life.

LEFT *An explosion of sunny color puts every cook in a good mood. The undeniable impact of this delightful kitchen relies on a strong color sense and an eye for display. Enameled advertising signs strike just the right note as wall decorations. The vibrant, clashing colors of the Fiestaware china celebrate color for its own sake.*

BELOW *A quintessentially 1950s look has been achieved here with a bright yellow and red color scheme and evocative textiles.*

STYLE ELEMENTS: RETRO DETAILS

1 Wicker furniture and rag rugs give the retro style a distinctly country feel.

2 Open shelves help create the look, and they also present the opportunity to display prized period pieces.

3 Every 1950s kitchen had at its heart a table. If it wasn't chrome and formica, then it was pine—sometimes with a zinc or enamel top—but almost always painted.

4, 5 Classic design abounded in the 1940s and '50s. The chrome-legged, upholstered bar stool is one such example.

Rustic

The revival of the rustic look signifies a return to basic values—there is no room here for anything laminated, cantilevered, or stainless. Surfaces are wood or stone, shelves are open, cupboards are freestanding, and the cook's equipment consists of a knife, a frying pan, a saucepan, and a mixing bowl. However, there is no need for inconvenience. Sinks and stoves can be both simple and efficient, and refrigerators and freezers can be hidden in utility rooms or behind cabinet doors, while rustic-looking paint finishes can be sealed for practicality. Rustic doesn't have to mean chaotic. Glass-fronted cabinets give the open look while keeping things under control, and hanging items from the walls or ceiling keeps counters clear from clutter.

LEFT *The low ceilings, beams, and pillars of this kitchen make the rustic scheme highly appropriate. Color is at the heart of the scheme, from the lilac-blue of the beaded-board wainscoting to the mellow yellow of the antique corner cupboard.*

RIGHT AND FAR RIGHT *The kitchen's exposed beams have been pressed into service, as they are just the right height for hanging pots, plate racks, baskets, and bunches of dried flowers. The painted wooden cabinets are based on simple, traditional designs.*

FAR LEFT *A simple country cupboard with a collection of country china and enamel. The little touches of yellow and blue bring it to life.*

LEFT *Sometimes it is best to leave distressed paintwork alone, as with this original country dresser that was made for a simple farmhouse kitchen.*

RIGHT *A magnificent mixing bowl sits on a sawbuck table now used as a work station. The armoire is used to store dry goods such as flour.*

Utilitarian objects, such as this metal laundry bowl, make perfect decorations for the rustic kitchen. If you are hanging them high up, then the objects should be large. Old farm implements are suitable as well.

Open plate racks are both traditional and practical, serving as both a drying rack and a storage facility. Drips from this rack splash onto a tiled countertop.

Antique cupboards and chests of drawers have been adapted to fit around a modern sink and appliances. The disparate elements are pulled together with a softly pigmented paint.

The freestanding furniture includes a simple painted wooden stool and a pretty double wicker basket with a distinctly homemade look.

RIGHT *The colorful face of the rustic kitchen: a stunning, blue-painted reproduction step-back cupboard. On the shelves is a collection of kitchen antiques: pantry boxes, firkins (covered buckets), and Shaker storage boxes.*

LEFT *Freestanding furniture is a key element of the rustic kitchen, while rag rugs and a wood-burning stove contribute to the effect, too. The walls would originally have been painted with a limewash, which allowed the walls to "breathe" and also kept insects at bay.*

RIGHT *An ad hoc look is much more in keeping than a carefully planned layout in the rustic kitchen.*

FAR RIGHT *The hutch is the focal point of many a rustic kitchen. Originally it stored everything from bread and cheese to knives and forks.*

CHAPTER THREE

Kitchen Living

A kitchen is the scene of many activities aside from cooking and doing the dishes. Given some thought, the hub of the house can become a workroom, a creative playroom, a family room, a casual diner, or a full-fledged formal dining room.

Coffee Corners

Unless you have a particularly small kitchen, try to include an area where you can enjoy a break from your labors, seat a guest with a glass of wine while you cook, or even dish up breakfast or a light lunch. All you need is a small table—it can be a foldaway—or a corner of countertop dedicated to sociable purposes and a couple of chairs or bar stools.

The area can double as a work space if you plan it that way from the outset, with electric outlets for a table lamp or a computer, wall space for a calendar and bulletin board, and a drawer for pens, pencils, day-planners, and telephone books.

LEFT *Time for a break in a corner of a small, rustic kitchen. A freestanding cupboard with fold-down flaps is the space-saving solution for an informal lunch.*

RIGHT *These bar stools reinterpret the classic bow-back Windsor chair, giving a vintage feel to this kitchen in a converted log barn. The custom-built cabinets have beaded-board detailing and maple countertops. The overhang allows the countertop to double as a convenient, space-saving breakfast bar.*

Breakfast bars and island counters create a sense of separation between cooking and eating and provide a pleasant environment for informal snacking away from the main traffic flow. The higher level also blocks the view of the messier aspects of food preparation. Bar stools,whether in the form of actual stools or of chairs with long legs, are available in every style imaginable, from the futuristic to the antique.

FAR LEFT *In this handsome converted barn, the kitchen occupies one end of the main room. The island unit with its built-in farmhouse sink separates the kitchen from the living area, and the raised breakfast bar hides the sink from general view.*

LEFT *From the living area, the view is of soaring architectural features, full-length windows, and beams, but nothing obviously kitchen-oriented. The breakfast bar is the dividing line between the two areas.*

Informal Dining

Why not eat in the kitchen? It is, after all, the room where the food is cooked, so it makes sense to eat it there. It is much friendlier, too, since the cook is not cut off from everyone else and the whole family can join in the preparation and the clearing up. With proper ventilation, cooking smells should not be a problem, and with intelligent lighting and sensible planning no one is going to be faced with the guilt-inducing sight of dirty pots and pans.

The dining kitchen should feel right for both types of activities. The kitchen must be inviting: this is not the place for harsh lighting or chipped sinks. And the dining area has to acknowledge that it is part of a working environment—you don't want it to look as if your elegant dining room furniture has been unceremoniously dumped in the kitchen.

RIGHT *This dining area at the far end of a traditional country kitchen filled with antique kitchenware is a storehouse of antique finds. The room gets its unique character from a salvaged corner cupboard with its display of old cans, a solid oak step-back cupboard, and a rare candle dryer in the corner.*

When a new kitchen is built on to a home, or internal walls are knocked down to create a larger space for the kitchen, portions of the old walls can sometimes be utilized to define separate areas within the new, open-plan room. The kitchen shown below and right in an addition is partially screened from the main living area by the center section of the original fireplace wall, allowing easy access from either side. A small eating area for two people is set in a cozy spot to one side of the fireplace. The chic, streamlined cabinets along the opposite wall are matched by the granite-topped center island, which turns the kitchen area into an efficient galley kitchen, and gives the fireside area a character of its own. The clean, cool neutrals of the kitchen—wood, stone, stainless steel, and white paint—are accented on one side by a wall of vibrant Navajo red, which gives the kitchen a lift and the intimate eating area a warm glow.

RIGHT AND BELOW *Just a few touches of Native American art in the form of rugs, throws, and a woven basket give this eating and sitting area a strong sense of identity. The simple, uncluttered line of the stone mantelpiece echoes the countertops. Candles and an intimate fireside freestanding lamp provide pools of ambient light after dark, while the work island is lit by stunning modern pendants.*

Shift the spotlight from one activity to another with flexible lighting controlled with dimmer switches.

Consider the view from every seat. Open shelves and glass-fronted cabinets make more interesting viewing than a row of blank cabinet doors.

Keep the style of decoration and furnishing of the two areas uniform throughout so that the different elements of the room work together.

Good ventilation is essential in the dining kitchen. An efficient vent hood will help eliminate cooking smells and steam.

Shield the view of dishes with a barrier.

Keep the table decorations fresh and simple. Big pitchers of flowers and overflowing bowls of fruit are much more suitable than ornate centerpieces and candelabra.

BELOW *A simple, white-painted table and chairs in front of an open window make a delightful breakfast area in this beach-house kitchen.*

1

2

KITCHEN ELEMENTS:
RELAXED DINING

1 Chrome and formica 1950s
   kitchen tables are the perfect
   size for an eat-in kitchen—
   they usually seat four or six
   in a pinch.

2 To add color and zing to a retro
   table setting, try to find vintage
   linens, plates, and glassware.

3 A change in flooring material can
   be very successful in giving the
   eating area a subtle distinction,
   particularly if you keep to
   sympathetic partnerships such
   as a coarse rug on hardwood.

3

The Formal Dining Area

For a formal dining area in a kitchen, a degree of separation is needed—otherwise, a beautifully set table twinkling with candlelight and crystal will look incongruous. If your kitchen is large, then a work island or peninsula is the answer, with kitchen activity on one side and dining on the other. In a smaller area, a judiciously placed half-wall with built-in narrow shelving can be used to block out kitchen messiness while allowing circulation between the two areas. Banishing wall cabinets and hanging up a few pictures will improve the view from the dining table.

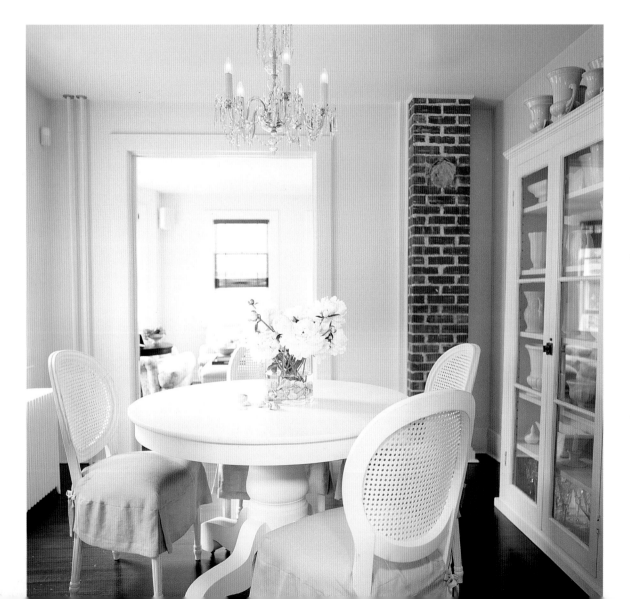

LEFT *A lovely pedestal table and nineteenth-century French bergère chairs make a delightful setting for dinner. The antique furniture is painted white so that it blends seamlessly with the white painted walls and exposed brickwork of this country kitchen. This elegant, tone-on-tone palette reinforces the formal aspect of this dining area. The dining end is given a further flourish with a chandelier.*

RIGHT *The simple, white-on-white theme continues with the decorative contents of the glass-fronted cabinet.*

With imagination, a kitchen and formal dining area can be made to complement each other beautifully. In this Federal-style 1820s sea captain's home, the cool, efficient kitchen leads through to a warm and intimate dining space that is part of it, but not within it.

Occupying the space formerly taken by a lean-to shed and a staircase, the dining area is separated from the kitchen by base cabinets and formal structural columns. The two areas are also demarcated by their color schemes and their flooring. On the kitchen side, the wood plank floor has been painted with a classic black-and-white diagonal tile design and bordered so it defines the kitchen area superbly.

ABOVE *The choice of white sink and white countertops helps the kitchen blend into the background so that attention is focused on the cozy yellow fireside dining room beyond.*

ABOVE *The dining furniture reinforces the antiquity of the house. The simple antique table and Windsor chairs are in perfect keeping with the style and furnishings of the entire room.*

ABOVE RIGHT *Attention to detail means this ceramic-tiled countertop doubles effortlessly as an elegant sideboard.*

The view from a formal dining area is important, whether it is a view of the garden or just the kitchen. Here the pristine white kitchen, with its classical columns and crisp black and white checkerboard floor complements the dining area splendidly.

Shared storage is a further advantage of a formal dining area adjacent to a kitchen. The beautifully finished custom-built cabinets between the two areas are accessed from both sides, so clean plates straight from the dishwasher go in one side and can be retrieved from the other when it is time to set the table. The cabinets also hold napkins, silverware, and serving dishes.

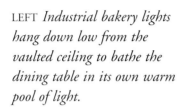

LEFT *Industrial bakery lights hang down low from the vaulted ceiling to bathe the dining table in its own warm pool of light.*

RIGHT *The view from the dining table is of a calm, tidy, well-ordered kitchen—an appetizing still life.*

In a very large kitchen, a formal dining area can make a strong visual statement, particularly if the table is in proportion to the size of the room. In some homes today, open-plan living, which combines kitchen, dining area, and living room in one large space, harks back to a time when a large home would have had a multifunctional great hall.

The interior architecture of the home pictured here evokes the wide open spaces of a freestanding barn. The kitchen is rich in Shaker-inspired details, and the dining area takes its cue from this. Ladder-back chairs with tape seats and shawl rails are placed around a tapered-leg pine farmhouse table. Simplicity and lightness prevail, aided by abundant natural light, warm wood tones, and muted Shaker colors.

To make the most of a semi-open-plan layout, the formal dining area pictured opposite is separated from the kitchen visually but not practically by a section of wall left standing when the room was remodeled. A large mirror hung on this wall prevents the dining space from feeling cramped. The farmhouse kitchen has been seamlessly updated to provide the best of traditional style alongside understated modern convenience. The range looks heartwarming and old-fashioned, but it is conveniently at the cutting edge of technology. The dining area is furnished with a simple antique pine table and traditional black painted Windsor chairs. Plain white walls and diagonally laid quarry tiles unite the two areas.

LEFT *The large, wood-framed mirror on the back wall bounces light around the room and provides a view of the garden from every seat at the table.*

RIGHT *Glass-fronted wall cabinets are made for the carefully organized contents to be admired. A microwave is installed unobtrusively beneath them. The farmhouse sink fits into the scheme perfectly, as do the wooden countertops.*

CHAPTER FOUR

Finishing Touches

When you are satisfied that your kitchen works well and there's a place for everything and everything is in its place, then it's time to add your own special touches, making the kitchen yours and yours alone. Remember, the details are what people often notice first.

Displaying Collections

Utilitarian household objects are often too beautiful to be hidden away behind closed cupboard doors. A shelf full of curvaceous pitchers or a collection of old enamel colanders can be as pleasing to look at as any work of art. Displaying the things you love is a great way to personalize your kitchen and create your own style.

Whatever your collection consists of, think of it less in terms of the individual pieces and more as a cohesive still life. Once you have pruned it and edited it, or even added to it, study each wall and countertop and work out the best way to create a "picture." You could install glass shelving, shelving units, glass-fronted cabinets, pegboard, or even a row of hooks to show off your possessions. The aim is to surprise and delight the eye.

LEFT *Everyday china in a mix-and-match rainbow of harmonizing colors was the idea behind American Fiestaware. Introduced in the 1930s and popular in the '50s, it is still widely collected and makes an excellent basis for a decorating scheme in the kitchen.*

RIGHT *Colorful china deserves to be admired on open shelves. This open unit adorns the wall like a painting.*

LEFT *When a collection depends on sheer numbers for its impact, cram the pieces together. If your collection is a little retro in feeling, find it a retro showcase. This 1920s tallboy is crammed with Fire King, a heat-proof oven-to-table glass that was all the rage in the 1940s. The fruit design on these Fire King casseroles, bowls, and cups and saucers is the most common of their hand-painted designs.*

TOP RIGHT *Jade-Ite items (some with their original boxes) are appropriately displayed in this 1950s cabinet.*

BOTTOM RIGHT *Jade-Ite piled up high in sculptural stacks.*

FAR RIGHT *A collection of mid-twentieth-century pitchers, teapots, and vases in a riot of bright colors, glossy finishes, and fascinating forms is housed in a modern industrial wire shelving unit—and looks wonderful.*

LEFT *A wonderfully battered hutch holds a unique collection of restaurant-weight cowboy-motif china.*

RIGHT *Chrome storage canisters and point-of-sale advertising material from the 1940s are displayed against a cherry red wall.*

Hutches are among the most adaptable, friendly, and useful pieces of furniture. They are also sometimes called dressers, from the French *dressoir,* which means a place to prepare, or dress, food. In early times a hutch consisted of a sideboard for doing this. To hold plates and dishes to accommodate the prepared food, it had drawers and cupboards beneath the worktop and later a low backboard fitted with shelves and more cupboards. Eventually, the low backboard became the tall rack found on today's hutch. Nowadays, the hutch is most likely to be used to display Grandma's china, but it will look particularly charming if you honor its origins by placing bowls of seasonal fruits and vegetables and other culinary delights alongside its more permanent contents.

LEFT *A rack filled with copper pans hangs above the work surface like a three-dimensional sculpture. In the glass-front cabinets, slip-glazed redware, chosen for its shape and pattern, mingles with jewel-toned glass.*

RIGHT *A collection of bold, utilitarian objects—burl-wood bowls, a cheese press, and three red apothecary tins—is juxtaposed with pumpkins and gourds to create an atmospheric kitchen still life.*

Collections of practical objects should be used as well as admired. Life's too short to hide away decorative china and bring it out for use only on special occasions. At any rate, plates that are often used are often washed and so do not accumulate dust and grease, which are hazards for all kitchen displays.

If you are going to show off your china, then choose a practical and attractive hutch with special grooves or beads on the shelves to hold plates safely and at the optimum angle. Avoid cluttering up the shelves with extraneous items or you will lose the impact. There may even be breakages as a result of, say, trying to extract a plate from behind a pile of household bills.

FAR LEFT *Hand-painted
Italian stoneware is displayed
in an early nineteenth-century
Irish hutch. The pattern's
universal color scheme looks
right whatever the time of
year, and these plates are used
regularly for dinner parties.*

LEFT *A pretty rose-patterned
tea service is complemented by
a pitcher of roses. It's a happy
juxtaposition that adds a
touch of freshness and wit.*

milk
bread
eggs
popcorn

LEFT *Functional objects double as design elements in this cool white kitchen where everything from spices and beans to everyday kitchenware is displayed with the care and attention normally given to rare collectibles.*

RIGHT *A collection of teapots and coffee pots is interspersed with small touches of silver and pewter.*

LEFT *Beneath the sign, a pretty shelf rack holds a collection of 1940s colored Fiesta glassware.*

RIGHT *A harlequin set of chairs surrounds a large pine farm table, giving this kitchen a welcoming feel. On the walls a profusion of chalkware fruit and vegetable plaques set the theme that inspired the color scheme.*

Making Your Kitchen Your Own

Now that all the practical decisions have been made, and your kitchen has been constructed and painted, it is time for you to take over. There is no one right way to decorate or accessorize the country kitchen, only the way that is right for you. So if you have passions, prepare to share them now. Whether you adore antiques or simply want to show off your treasured china, the details finish off the room and make it feel like a part of your home.

A jolt of sunshine is what the owners of this idiosyncratic kitchen set out to achieve. They created a welcoming, cheerful jumble using fruit and flower motifs in profusion, providing a natural complement to the cheery, bright color scheme and to the garden views captured by two walls of windows. The distinctly 1950s feeling is reinforced by the casual gingham window treatments with their bow trims as well as by the period enamelware and mid-twentieth-century pottery that is the color of lemons, limes, and tangerines.

Serious works of art have no real place in a kitchen. Moisture and grease do not create the right atmosphere for oil paintings, and even pictures behind glass must be properly sealed and kept away from the stove.

Instead, seize the opportunity to create a work of art of your own. Make glorious still life arrangements of flowers, fruits, and vegetables or exploit the sculptural possibilities of kitchen utensils. There are so many textures and forms to play with, from delicate wire egg baskets to rustic wooden gingerbread molds, and there's color in those kitchen antiquities, from the brilliant flash of a copper gelatin mold to the dull sheen of a well-used muffin pan.

LEFT *One bread bin is just a bread bin, but a whole heap of them is a work of art. These English enamelware bread and flour bins make a graphic retro statement.*

RIGHT *Cake, muffin, and popover pans adorn the walls of this kitchen, resembling bas-relief plaques.*

KITCHEN ELEMENTS: DISPLAY

1 Herbs, both medicinal and culinary, are stored in a glass-fronted antique cabinet. The neat rows are useful as well as decorative.

2 Antiques found in flea markets can make wonderful collections for kitchens. Displayed here on rustic shelves are a selection of graters, a maple syrup tin, and, on the top shelf, a colorful egg grader.

3 A kitchen with a 1950s flavor has at its heart a refurbished 1949 wedgewood stove. The loosely matched collection of jars and cans reinforces the 1950s theme. Collections should evolve, which means retiring some items and welcoming others.

4 A serious collection of nineteenth-century wooden potato mashers, known as beetles. It looks like an art installation celebrating the curvaceous profiles of these old-fashioned turned-wood tools.

5 The large landscape painting makes a natural focal point, drawing attention to a utilitarian composition of antique white enamelware.

Tea bags
Branston
    Pickle
Aubergines
Wine
Bird seed

Feed the cat

Jayne.
Pick up Charlie
@ 2pm!

Call Ivana

Dinner with
Howard and
Madison - Sat.

ask Buddy to
pick up the Bodes
for Emma.

ADMIRAL

FAR LEFT *A practical bulletin board. In this cheerful family kitchen two panels of the cupboard door were painted with latex chalkboard paint.*

CENTER *A still life massed on the top of a retro-style refrigerator.*

LEFT *A bread and pizza oven tucked into a brick alcove is topped with a basket of flowers.*

Decorative paint effects offer a great deal of scope for improving a kitchen, either subtly or dramatically, whether you do them yourself or commission a paint-effects specialist. Wooden cabinets and worktops can be given a time-worn look with distressing or a crackle glaze, a kitchen door could be wood-grained, a tabletop marbleized, and cupboard doors and drawers painted with trompe l'oeil scenes ranging from still lifes of fruits and flowers to full-scale murals of animals or landscapes.

Paint effects have certainly made all the difference to this kitchen, in which the owner has gone all out for the pastoral look. Trompe l'oeil scenes painted on the cupboards evoke an idyllic farmscape picturesquely populated by cows, horses, goats, geese, and pigs.

Because the kitchen is large, the near life-size scale of the paintings is not a problem. The fact that the animals appear to be glimpsed through the panels of cupboard doors fuels the illusion that the animals, and the lovely summer's day, are just outside the kitchen.

LEFT AND FAR LEFT *Trompe l'oeil horses and geese graze outside the pantry and a goat guards the refrigerator door. Contrasting red trim highlights the portraiture as well as the fine cabinetwork. A golden overglaze was added to simulate an aged look.*

RIGHT *Decorative paint effects can instantly change the ambience of a room. Here a brand-new wooden kitchen cabinet has been distressed and crackle-glazed, taking the kitchen back in time.*

1

2

3

FLOWERS AND PLANTS

Tucked into china displays or sitting atop windowsills or shelves, house plants, flowers, and fresh herbs give a kitchen an injection of fresh, colorful contrast among all the hard surfaces.

1 A sunny corner of the kitchen is the perfect place to display a truly stunning floral arrangement.

2, 3 You don't have to put flowers into conventional vases—look for unusual and appropriate containers. Old or damaged china can find a new life as a receptacle for blooms, but do not reuse them for food or drinks.

4 An old galvanized bucket adds a rustic feel to a country kitchen.

5 Colorful fruits and vegetables are a natural for a kitchen display, and fruits in particular are sweeter to eat when served at room temperature than when taken straight from the refrigerator.

6 Egg cups are perfect for displaying single flowers in full bloom. Grow herbs in a sunny windowsill and keep cut herbs in pitchers near the cooktop. Apart from the wonderful aromas, a touch of green can whet the appetite.

Index